This edition published 2004 by
Mercury Books
20 Bloomsbury Street
London WC1B 3JH
ISBN 1-904668-70-4
Copyright © 2003 Allegra Publishing Ltd

Publisher: Felicia Law
Design director: Tracy Carrington
Project manager: Karen Foster
Author: Gerry Bailey
Editor: Rosalind Beckman
Designed by: Jacqueline Palmer
assisted by Fanny Level, Will Webster
Cartoon illustrations: Steve Boulter (Advocate)
and Andrew Keylock (Specs Art Agency)
Make-and-do: Jan Smith
Model-maker: Tim Draper
further models: Robert Harvey, Abby Dean
Photo studio: Steve Lumb
Photo research: Diana Morris
Scanning: Acumen Colour
Proof-reading: Victoria Grimsell
Digital workflow: Edward MacDermott

Printed by D 2 Print Singapore

Crafty Inventions

EARLY DISCOVERIES

Contents

Mercury Junior
20 BLOOMSBURY STREET
LONDON WC1B 3JH

How can I find my way at sea?

Robert is the navigator of a ship that has been blown off-course by a hurricane. He can no longer see the shore and he has no idea how far north or south he has sailed. He must find his bearings if the ship is to get back on course.

Robert has only enough food and water to last a few days. He must head in the right direction at once or the food will run out before the ship can reach land.

The ship's astromomer can't think what to do. He just draws triangles.

If he heads the wrong way, he might fall off the edge of the world. Or he might just sail around in circles. Both possibilities sound dreadful.

> I must learn how to navigate the ship in open waters.

WHAT CAN HE DO?

- He could follow a school of dolphins and hope they swim in a straight line towards land.

- He could send out the ship's talking parrot. When it returns, it might tell him the position of the ship.

- When night falls, he could ask the ship's astronomer to look at the stars. The night sky might act like a map and show where the ship is.

- The astronomer says he needs to compare a star's position above the horizon to its position when he was on land - a calculation he already knows.

I'll make a disc with all 360 degrees of a circle marked around its edge. If I fix a pointer to the middle, I can calculate the angle between the star, the ship and the horizon. I can then calculate how high the star is above the horizon – and compare its position at sea with its position on land.

An astrolabe was an important navigating instrument that used the stars to fix a ship's position when travelling east-west.

Navigator's tool

An **astrolabe** is an instrument used by navigators and astronomers to measure the **altitude**, or height, of the Sun, a star or planet above the **horizon**. It is made up of a circular disc marked with a scale that measures 360 degrees around its rim.

At the centre of the disc is a moveable arm. Astronomers would hold the disc **vertically** to the horizon and point the arm at a particular star or planet. Once the position of the star or planet was known, the position of a ship could be easily calculated.

Astronomy

Astronomy is the scientific study of everything that exists in the **Universe** outside the atmosphere of our Earth. Most scientists study a specific area of astronomy. Some study the stars, others study our entire solar system – the Sun and the planets that orbit it. Others study the origins of the universe and try to work out how it began.

The first great astronomer was the Greek scientist, Ptolemy. He lived in Alexandria in Egypt in the second century AD. Ptolemy thought that our planet Earth was at the centre of the Universe – an idea that did not change for over 1000 years after Ptolemy died. However, Ptolemy's great contribution was to work out the movements of the planets. He made a catalogue of 1022 stars and grouped them into 48 star patterns, known as **constellations**.

EYE-STRONOMY

Unlike modern astronomers who work with very powerful instruments, the first star gazers used only the naked eye to study the stars.

The Babylonians had charted the pattern and movement of stars and planets by 450 BC. The ancient Egyptians used the position of the star Sirius to predict the coming of spring.

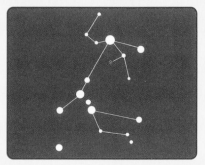

Ptolemy's model of the Universe shows the Earth as a stationery planet with the Sun, Moon and other stars and planets moving around it.

Inventor's words

altitude • astrolabe
astronomy
constellation
horizon • Universe
vertical

Make your own astrolabe

You will need

- thick card
- coloured paper
- scissors • wire
- protractor
- rope

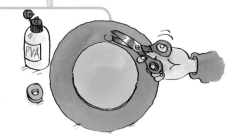

1 Cut a circle of thick card, then stick it on to a larger circle of thinner coloured paper. Cut out hole at the top of paper disc for the handle.

Central measurement arm

2 Cut out the central measurement arm in this shape.

3 Fix the central measurement arm to the centre of the card disc centre with strong wire.

4 Using your protractor, mark 360 degrees around the card disc.

5 Decorate your astrolabe. Tie on a piece of rope for the handle.

HOW TO USE YOUR ASTROLABE

1. Choose a sunny day and hold your astrolabe by the loop at the top, letting it hang down.

2. Turn it edge-on to the Sun and adjust the arm so that there is no shadow - this is when the arm is pointing directly at the Sun.

3. You will see that the arm will point to different numbers at different times of the day and at different times of the year.

4. Take measurements 90 degrees from the Sun.

How can I spin wool quickly?

Lila has an order from the prince for 100 shirts. They have to be finished in a week or she will lose the job. But she cannot spin enough yarn in that time by hand. She may have to turn the job down.

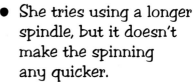

Lila has enough wool to spin 100 shirts. But she must first turn the wool into thread so the shirts can be woven.

Lila always uses a notched stick called a spindle and a bowl called a whorl to spin. But it is slow work.

All the other women in the village are busy, so she has no help. Even if she spins all night, she will not make enough thread.

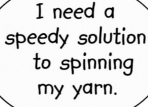

I need a speedy solution to spinning my yarn.

WHAT CAN SHE DO?

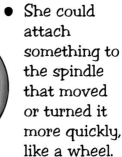

- She could teach her pet monkey, Pepe, to use a spindle. But would he sit still long enough?

- She tries using a longer spindle, but it doesn't make the spinning any quicker.

- She could attach something to the spindle that moved or turned it more quickly, like a wheel.

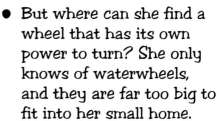

- But where can she find a wheel that has its own power to turn? She only knows of waterwheels, and they are far too big to fit into her small home.

I'll fit an old cartwheel to the spindle. The wheel will twist the spindle round at great speed as it turns. I can connect a pedal to the wheel and press it to make the wheel turn. It'll be less tiring than turning the wheel by hand.

Today, most fibres are spun in factories, but some traditional societies still use a spinning wheel.

Spinning wheel

Spinning is one of the two processes involved in making cloth. Spinning prepares the fibre by twisting and drawing it out into a long yarn, or thread; weaving makes the thread into a sheet of cloth. Spinners first used a revolving spindle, which they rolled against their leg.

In about 500 BC in India, a wheel was used for the first time to turn the **spindle**. The spindle was connected to the large wheel by a belt, or drive band. It was known as a great wheel, and was the first spinning device to use a mechanised spindle. Spinning was women's work, carried out from home.

9

Wheel and axle

A **wheel and axle** is one of the six simple machines that make work easier. It is made up of a round wheel with an axle that sticks through its **hub**, or centre. The wheel and axle turn together. They turn round an imaginary line, called an **axis**, that runs through the middle of the hub.

When two wheels are attached to an axle, one at each end, the device can be used to make a rolling wagon or other type of vehicle. But a single wheel and axle can also be used to do work. A large wheel increases the amount of twisting force that goes through the axle. A door knob works in this way.

WHEEL OR LEVER?

The wheel and axle is actually both a wheel and a lever. The centre of the axle does the same job as a fulcrum in a lever. The radius of the axle is the load arm, while the radius of the wheel is the force or effort.

A wheel and axle is also used to draw water out of a well. A rope attached to a bucket is wound around the axle. The wheel is turned by a handle to raise or lower the bucket.

A wheel and axle device makes it easy to lift heavy buckets of water from a well.

Inventor's words

axis • hub
spindle
wheel and axle

Make a cotton wool bracelet

You will need

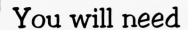

- cotton wool
- paint • felt tip or marker pens
- silver foil

1 Take a ball of cotton wool and gently pinch a small piece between your fingers.

2 Roll it between your finger and thumb, gently twisting all the time until you make a fine string.

3 Keep going – you can twist in cotton wool from a fresh ball – until you have a string about 30cm long. Now make several of these strings.

4 Colour the strings using paint or markers. When the strings are dry, plait them to make a multi-coloured cord.

5 Join 2 or 3 of these cords together and decorate them with twists of silver foil to make an attractive bracelet.

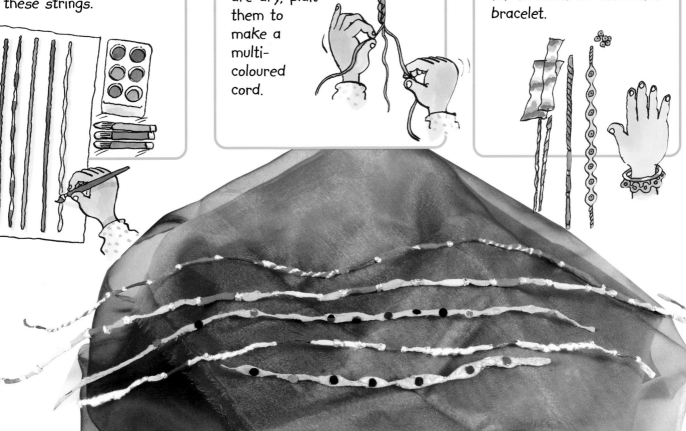

How can I steer my boat?

Another steering oar has broken and now Wu Yee cannot steer his boat. To make matters worse, the wind is changing direction all the time and he is sailing round in circles. He must find a better way of steering his boat.

Wu Yee has a rich cargo of spices and other foods on board. But if he is blown off-course and loses any more time, the food will spoil and he'll not be paid for all his hard work.

Oars are fine to use in calm seas. But in a rough sea, they are in danger of snapping.

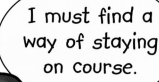

I must find a way of staying on course.

WHAT CAN HE DO?

- He could make his steering oars out of iron. But they would be too heavy - and likely to rust.

- He could steer with his sails, furling and unfurling them to catch the wind correctly. But what if the wind dies down?

- He could rely on his oarsmen, but he must make sure the strongest rowers don't turn the boat in one direction.

- He could nail an oar on to the front of the boat. The water pushing against it equally on both sides should keep it and the boat straight.

Aha! I will adapt a steering oar to make a rudder. A piece of wood at the back of the boat will swivel from side to side as the water pushes against it, and will help turn the boat left or right. I will attach a handle to control it.

The invention of the rudder made steering boats easier.

Easy steering

A **rudder** is part of the steering mechanism of a boat or ship. A ship's rudder is a flat piece of wood or metal that sticks out from the **stern** of the ship. A rudder can be moved to left or right, using its handle, called the tiller. The **tiller** steers the ship in the opposite direction to its movement.

So, if the captain moves the tiller to the right, the flowing water will push against the left side of the rudder blade. This then pushes the stern of the ship to the right – and the front, or **bow**, of the ship to the left. Today, most modern ships use a wheel, called a **helm**, to steer, and not a tiller.

Equilibrium

Equilibrium occurs when an object is completely still and balanced. When two or more forces of equal strength push against an object from opposite directions, we say that the object is in equilibrium.

When we are sitting on a chair, for example, the force of **gravity**, the force that pulls us to Earth, presses us down on to it. At the same time, the chair we sit in is strong enough to hold us up. The strength of the chair pushing up produces a force equal to the force of gravity pushing down. Because the two forces are equal, we are in equilibrium.

IN THE BALANCE

With a set of scales, if there is nothing in the pan, the arm will balance on its centre or pivot, so both sides are an equal distance from the table. The scales are in equilibrium. If you put a weight in the pan that is equal to the weight at the other end of the arm, you keep the equilibrium.

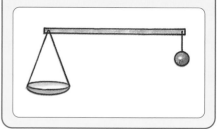

If one of the chair legs snapped, however, the force of the chair would become less. Equilibrium, or the balance of forces would be broken, and gravity would pull us down to the floor.

By maintaining their equilibrium, acrobats can balance on top of each other without falling.

Inventor's words

bow
equilibrium
helm • gravity
rudder
stern • tiller

Make a model boat

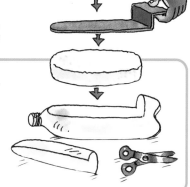

You will need

- plastic drinks bottle
- scissors
- card • polystyrene
- glue • thin sticks
- hooks and eyes
- string • wire • cork
- paper or light cloth
coloured paper • paint

1 Cut away one side of a plastic bottle to make the hull of your boat. Cut a piece of card for the deck and a chunk of polystyrene to fill the space underneath.

2 Make a rudder from 2 pieces of card glued together and a stick for a handle. Fix hooks to the rudder to hinge it to the stern (back) of the boat. Bind the handle with string.

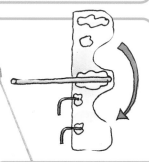

3 Make two holes in the stern and fit 2 eyes. Join the hooks and eyes to connect the rudder to the deck of the boat. Add a card rail for the handle of the rudder.

4 Fix the mast and boom together with wire or string, so that they move easily. Glue a cork to the deck. Push the mast down through a cork and into the deck. Add a cloth or paper sail.

How can I see inside my castle?

Mung has moved into a new castle. He likes it but the rooms are too dark. The narrow openings don't let in much light. And larger ones let in the cold, and must be covered. He must brighten up his new home quickly before he runs out of candles.

At night, Mung uses torches to light his rooms. But he can't have torches lit during the day as well. It's too dangerous with all the straw on the ground. Anyway, the torches burn quickly. He would need a huge supply.

How can I brighten up my fine new home?

He could count his money by candlelight, but he might strain his eyes. He also needs light to keep other parts of the castle clean. Mung likes a neat, tidy castle with all the dark corners swept.

WHAT CAN HE DO?

- He could ask his servants to stand in front of the openings when the wind blows, then move aside when it stops.

- He could ask his wife to knit coverings to keep the wind out. But the rooms would be even darker.

- Some kind of transparent, or clear, material would be ideal. But what kind? Some animal skins are transparent, but they are not strong enough to keep the wind out.

- The glass that his friend, Tip, uses for making pots is transparent. Perhaps he should talk to Tip.

I'll measure the openings and then ask Tip to make flat sheets of glass of a similar size. Then I'll put each sheet in a wooden frame and fix it inside the opening. The window will allow plenty of light to come through, but block out the wind.

Glass is shaped while it is soft. It quickly hardens as it cools.

Sheets of glass

Glass is a hard, clear substance made from the minerals sand, soda and lime. These minerals are heated until they **fuse**, or melt together. The fusing together, or **fusion**, of these minerals makes glass. Flat glass is used for most windows, but it was not invented until long after glass itself had first been used to make small pots, vases or wine holders. Flat glass was first made by blowing a bubble of **molten** glass then spinning it until it was flat. This made small sheets of glass with a little bump in the middle, which is known as crown glass. The flat glass round the bump was cut into window panes.

Melting point

The **melting point** is the temperature at which a substance changes from a solid to a liquid. Different solids have different melting points. For example, the melting point of ice is 0° Celsius. The melting point of steel is much higher, about 1500° Celsius.

BOILING POINT

The melting point of a substance can change if the pressure of the air around it changes. If the air pressure rises around water, its melting and boiling points get lower. A pressure cooker raises the pressure of the air inside it, which raises the boiling point. This makes the food cook much faster.

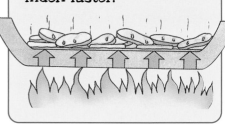

Any substance will melt if it is heated to its own particular melting point temperature. **Mixtures** of substances melt over a range of temperatures, depending on the proportion of their contents. Mixtures like glass do not simply melt. They also become softer as the temperature gets higher. So glass can be heated until it becomes sticky like toffee and easy to work with.

Where the ice is melting, the temperature is 0° Celsius.

Inventor's words

glass • fuse
fusion
melting point
mixture
molten

Make a sun screen

You will need
- card • scissors
- lightweight paper
- glue • pipe cleaners
- paint or felt tips pens

1 Take a piece of card and cut out a window shape. Your window can be square, rectangular or diamond-shaped.

2 Fix 2 card hinges on to one side of the window.

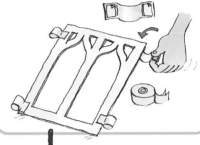

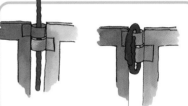

3 Take a piece of lightweight paper. Fold in half again and again.

4 Snip out a pattern. Open out and glue to the frame of the window. Decorate the front with paint or felt tips.

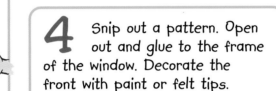

5 Join the windows together with pipe cleaners to make a screen.

Place in front of a window and look at the patterns of light 19

How can I find my way?

Marcus has been away from his village for days. He was sent up into the hills to find a new source of water. He has travelled a long way to find it, but now he is lost and cannot find his way back home in the dark.

He knows he has to go south to hit the village, but the sky is cloudy and he cannot see the stars.

He is so hungry, he pours some cold soup into a bowl and rummages in his bag for a spoon. But, instead, he pulls out a splinter of metal, which drops into his soup.

He watches as the needle-shaped splinter floats in the soup and slowly swivels round. When it stops, it points to a clump of trees nearby. Idly, he drops the metal in again – it turns and points the same way.

I wonder why the metal splinter always points in the same direction.

WHAT CAN HE DO?

- Roll down the hill and hope he reaches his village in one piece!

- Wait for morning and use the rising Sun in the east as his guide. But it could rain all week, which would block out the Sun.

- Look for a familiar tree or hill to fix a direction. Yes, fixing a direction is good.

- What about the soup and the metal splinter? Perhaps he should think about this a little longer.

No matter how I hold my bowl, the metal splinter always points in the same direction. And now that the Sun is out, I can see that the splinter always points north-south. I'll carry the bowl carefully so the metal needle floats freely, and follow a southerly direction all the way home. Look, I've made a compass!

A modern compass is housed in a case, marked with all the directions.

The first compass

The metal ore Marcus found was first discovered in Asia in ancient times. It was a magnetic material called **magnesium**. In Europe, an oblong piece of magnesium was sometimes tied to a string to point north and south. It was called a 'leading' stone, which later became **'lodestone'**. The first compass made use of a sliver of magnetic material. It was placed on a piece of cork and floated on a pan of water.

The letters for north, south, east and west – called the cardinal points – were painted on the side. A modern **compass** is fixed to a base by a pivot, which allows the needle to spin. It spins to point north and south whenever the compass is moved. A compass card has the cardinal points written on it. In between the cardinal points are the intercardinal points: north-east, north-west, south-east and south-west.

Giant magnet

Our Earth has a ball-shaped centre, or inner core. Scientists believe it is made up of solid iron and another metal called nickel. Iron is magnetic, which means that it attracts other metals. In this way, the Earth acts like a giant magnet. Scientists draw an imaginary line that runs through the Earth's centre. At opposite ends of the line there is a north **magnetic pole** and a south magnetic pole. We call these the north and south **poles**.

Any metals that are mined from our planet will also be magnetic, some more than others. Even the smallest piece will also have a north and south pole and will always point in the same direction as the Earth's poles. A bar **magnet** has the poles at each end.

As the Earth spins round, the poles always point in the same direction.

THE EARTH'S POLES

Earth's magnetic force is strongest near its poles, but the force also stretches far into space. The Moon, for example, circles Earth daily, and is held by its magnetic force.

North Pole

South Pole

Inventor's words

compass
iron
lodestone
magnesium
magnet
magnetic pole
pole

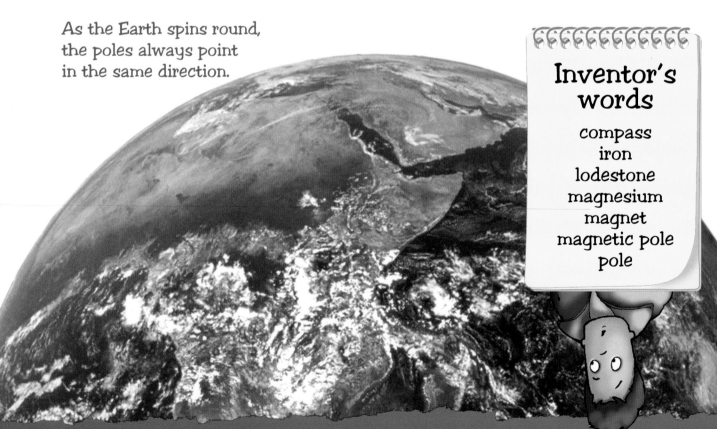

22

Make a floating compass

You will need
- round margarine tub lid
- polystyrene pizza base
- paint • glue
- bar magnet
- bottle end
- different-coloured straws
- string
- double-sided tape

1 Glue the tub lid to the centre of the pizza base. Paint or decorate the lid with a picture of the world. Fix a marked north–south bar magnet to the centre of the lid.

2 Cover the lid picture and magnet with the bottle end.

3 Cut the different-coloured straws into small pieces and glue around the polystyrene pizza base.

4 Roll the string on to double-sided tape to make 4 mats, one for each direction. With the straws, make a N, S, E and W for each mat and stick on to the compass.

USING YOUR COMPASS

Fill a plastic bowl with water and gently place the compass on the surface. It will spin round for a moment and then settle, indicating north and south.

Remember to keep magnets away from metal objects

How can I count up quickly?

Kim is a peddler. He has to take his goods to the town to sell. But he is worried about how to add up and subtract his prices. In his yard, he can draw columns in the earth and use pebbles to do his calculations. But he can't take his yard to town!

Kim has loaded his ribbons and rolls of silk on to his donkey. They are the best quality so he can ask high prices for them.

But he can't calculate the price in his head and he just doesn't have enough fingers.

I must find a speedier way of doing more difficult sums.

He could guess at a high price and hope his customers will pay. But he might get it wrong and make enemies. Or he could lower his price, but then he would make a loss.

WHAT CAN HE DO?

- He could take a large tub of earth with him, and a sack of pebbles. He'd look pretty silly, but at least he'd have his counting machine at hand!

- He could take his clever cousin Pomot with him. But can he trust Pomot not to cheat?

- He thought of his wife's necklace. Perhaps he could thread beads on to a string and use them to count.

- Then he saw his harp sitting in a corner. The harp had not just one string, but several. That gave him an idea.

I'll fix wires with beads strung on them into a wood frame. Each wire will represent a number beginning with 1-9. Other wires can hold beads for higher numbers. Then I'll be able to count across the columns of beads.

You can add, subtract, multiply and divide on an abacus.

Counting frame

An **abacus** is a device used for counting and doing arithmetic. It was invented thousands of years ago in different parts of the world. The ancient Babylonians, Egyptians and Chinese all used the abacus. When the Spanish discovered America in the 1500s, they saw that the Maya people of Central America had also invented and used an abacus.

An abacus is made up of a frame holding rows of beads strung on wires. The beads are moved along the wires to add or subtract. Multiplication is done by repeated addition, while division is done by repeated subtraction. Some Asian merchants still use the abacus to count. They can work out their sums faster than a modern calculator.

1 to 10

In ancient times, different peoples used different marks to stand for **numerals**, or the symbols that represent each number. The Egyptians used pictures, while the Romans used shapes rather like fingers and hands. The numerals we use were invented in India about 2000 years ago.

The Arab peoples adopted these numerals and brought them to Europe, where they became known as Arabic numerals. **Arabic numerals** are more useful than Roman numerals for doing written arithmetic because they are easier to use.

Using the Arabic system, the value of a number depends on its position in a column of numbers. This is called **place value**.

ZERO

About 1500 years ago, the Hindus in India invented a new numeral to stand for the empty place on an abacus wire. They called it 'sunya', or 'nothing'. With nine numerals and sunya, they could write any number. The Arabs called this numeral 'sifr' and wrote it as 'O'. Our word 'zero' comes from 'sifr'.

O

The first number in the column in this system stands for ones, or **units**. The second number represents tens, the third stands for hundreds, and so on. Place value makes arithmetic easier to do on paper.

This early calendar uses Arabic numerals.

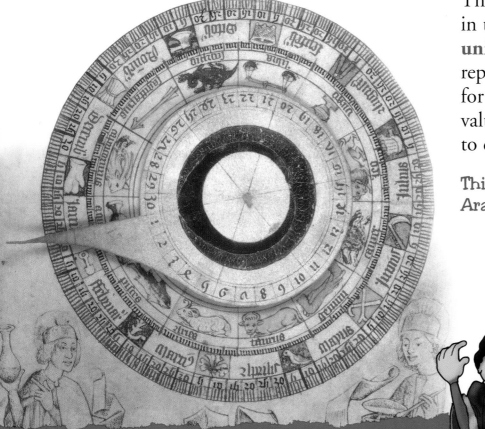

Inventor's words

abacus
Arabic numerals
numerals
place value
units

Make your own abacus

You will need
- thick card
- femo moulding clay
- 6 kebab sticks
- 6 corks

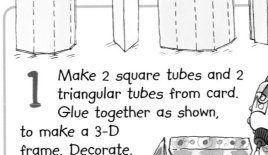

1 Make 2 square tubes and 2 triangular tubes from card. Glue together as shown, to make a 3-D frame. Decorate.

2 When dry, push 6 kebab sticks through one end of the frame, at equal distances from each other.

3 Make coloured femo beads with holes in. Bake to harden.

4 Thread the beads on to the sticks – 2 on to each stick, followed by a cardboard divider, and then another 5 beads to make a total of 7.

5 Glue corks on to the base of the frame and push the sticks into them to secure. Trim the sticks at the top of the frame and glue in place.

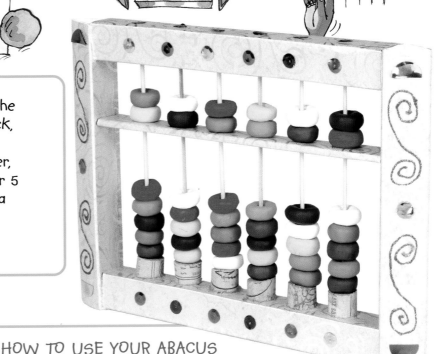

HOW TO USE YOUR ABACUS

1. Place the abacus flat on the table with the rows of 2 beads at the top.

2. From right to left, the first column is for single units, the next is the tens column, etc. Beads in the upper section have a value of 5; beads in the lower section have a value of 1.

3. Begin counting by pushing the lower beads towards the bar in the centre.

4. Instead of counting the fifth unit by pushing the fifth bead up to the centre, substitute one of the top beads by pushing it down towards the centre to represent the number five.

See how fast you can add up your shopping bill

How can I copy things?

Liliana wants to be able to paint wonderful pictures like her brother, Carlo. But she is a girl and not allowed to attend the painting school with her brother. Also, she fears she may not be skilled in copying the things she sees around her.

Liliana cannot get trees to look like trees or the cat to look like the cat. She knows it is easier to trace an image to get a good copy, but she can only do this with flat objects.

Whatever can I use to make perfect copies?

She watches the shadows play on the wall. The sunshine outlines lots of objects. The cat's outline is perfect when the sunshine makes it.

WHAT CAN SHE DO?

- She could dress up as a boy and go to Maestro Giorgio's copying lessons. But she's bound to be found out.

- She could trace around any object as long as it was flat. But some things are just too big.

- What if she held up an old canvas to catch the shadow of a vase on a table? But the canvas has a hole in the middle so the shadow is not perfect.

- But she notices something else. The light passing through the hole has made an exact image of the vase on the wall behind. The only thing is, the image is upside down.

That's it! I'll direct the upside-down image on to another canvas instead of the wall. Then I can copy it and turn the canvas the right way up. If I cover the space between the canvases I might *be able to* make the image clearer.

L. Cossinus

Camera obscura is Latin for a 'dark room'. Many of the first camera obscuras were large rooms used for observing a solar eclipse.

Picturing things

The first camera obscuras were used by astronomers, but by the 17th century many artists used them. A **camera obscura** works in the same way as an ordinary camera. Light from an object passes through a small hole in the surface of a box, or even the wall of a room, and creates an image, or copy, on any flat surface a short distance away.

Light usually travels in straight lines, so the light from the bottom of the object passes up and through the small hole to make the top of the **image**. The light from the top of the object passes through the hole and continues downwards to make the bottom of the image. The image is upside down, but forms a perfect copy of the object.

Lightwaves

Light is a form of energy. Light energy moves in waves, travelling at a very high speed. In deep space, far outside Earth's atmosphere, the speed of light is 299,792 km per second. Light travels in straight lines most of the time, but it bends when it travels from one substance to another. It can also bend around the edge of an object.

We see objects when light from them enters our eyes. Natural objects such as the Sun and man-made ones such as lightbulbs, emit, or give out, their own light. They are known as sources of light. Other objects, such as the Moon and mirrors, **reflect** light, which means that light from another source bounces back off them.

The shape of lightwaves can be clearly seen as sunlight falls through the trees.

REFLECTIONS

When you stand in front of a mirror, light bounces off you, passes through the mirror's glass and bounces straight back off the shiny layer behind.

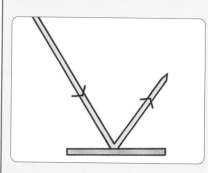

You see yourself as a reflection. But because the light reflects straight back at you, your left hand is shown as the right hand of the image in the mirror.

Inventor's words

camera obscura
image
lightwaves
reflect

Make a pin-hole camera

This simple device shows exactly how a camera lens works

You will need

- small cardboard box, about 20cm x 10cm x 10cm or piece of cardboard
- thin plastic lid or piece of thin card
- thumbtack
- clear or opaque plastic bag
- tape • glue • paint

1 If you cannot find a suitably-sized box, you can make one by folding and glueing cardboard. Leave the box open at one end.

2 At the closed end, cut a hole smaller than the plastic lid – this is where the lens is going to be. Make a hole in the plastic lid with a thumbtack, then glue the lid over the hole.

3 Stretch a piece of plastic bag tightly over the open end of the box to make your viewing screen, and tape securely.

4 Fold and glue a piece of card around the camera so that the screen is well shaded, and glue to the camera. Paint and decorate your camera.

HOW TO USE YOUR PINHOLE CAMERA

Go outside on a sunny day and look through the hole in your camera. The plastic makes a screen that shows you upside-down colour pictures.

How can I send a message?

Tang and two fellow soldiers are sent by the general to scout the enemy line. They have to find out how many men the enemy army has and where they are located.

Trooper Tang scratches his head. He needs to get an urgent message to his general but there is a company of enemy troops on the hill between Tang and the general, and no way of getting the message through.

> I must find a way of sending a message without risking my life.

Tang cannot skirt around the enemy line as it will take too long. He thinks about splitting up with his companions and making a run through the middle. But that will mean certain death.

WHAT CAN HE DO?

- He could tape a message to the legs of a bird and hope it flies in the right direction.

- Digging a tunnel under the enemy. lines might work. But by the time he finished, the battle would be over!

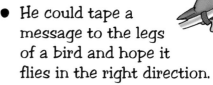

- What if he hoisted a flag with his message written on it? If he held it high enough the general might just see it. But the flag would need to be very high.

- Perhaps he could tie his flag on to a very long piece of string. The wind would help the flag to fly high, but would he be able to control it?

I'll gather some twigs and make a frame in the shape of a cross, with one arm longer than the other. Then I'll stretch a cloth over the frame and tie on a long piece of string.

The Chinese fly kites of many colours and shapes.

Up high

A **kite** is a kind of aircraft. It is made of material such as cloth or paper that is stretched over a frame. A kite uses the force of the wind to fly. It is guided from the ground by a long cord, or the kite's tail.

The first kites were probably invented by the Chinese over 2000 years ago. These kites were used for military purposes such as sending messages. Today, special kites are used to carry measuring devices into the atmosphere.

Wind energy

Wind energy describes how the movement of the wind is used to make a machine work. Windmills use wind energy to push round the sails, which then turn the wheels that grind the corn. Sailing ships use wind energy to push against the sails and move the ship forwards.

Moving things such as wind or water have energy that can be used to power something else. This kind of energy is called **kinetic energy**. Kinetic comes from the Greek word for 'move'. All moving things have kinetic energy.

POTENTIAL ENERGY

Even things that are not moving have a kind of energy. An apple in a tree may not be moving. But it could move. When it is ripe, it will probably drop to the ground. An apple on a tree is said to have a kind of energy known as potential energy.

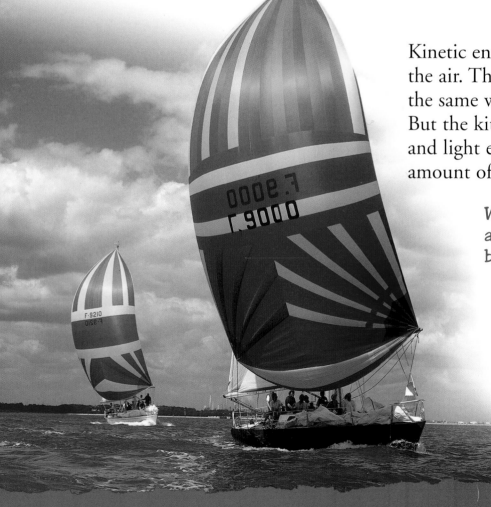

Kinetic energy allows a kite to stay in the air. The wind pushes the kite in the same way as it pushes a ship's sail. But the kite must be wide enough and light enough to catch the right amount of wind to get a good push.

Wind energy can power anything from a paper bag to a yacht.

Inventor's words

kinetic energy
kite
potential energy
wind energy

Let's go fly a kite!

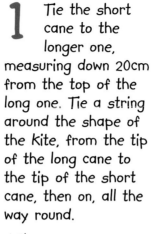

You will need

- 2 light canes –
40cm and 60cm
- string • scissors
- bright wrapping paper
- glue • paperclips
- tape

1 Tie the short cane to the longer one, measuring down 20cm from the top of the long one. Tie a string around the shape of the kite, from the tip of the long cane to the tip of the short cane, then on, all the way round.

2 Lay the frame on a sheet of wrapping paper and draw round it, leaving a flap about 2cm wider than the shape of the kite. Cut the paper out and fix to the frame by folding the flap over and glueing it.

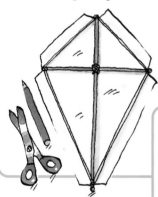

3 Measure in halfway from the tip of the cross to the centre on each side and carefully fix a length of string about 40 cm long to these 2 points. Knot a paperclip or wire loop to the centre of this string. This makes the harness to which you attach your flying string.

4 Make a tail for your kite by knotting paper bows at intervals along a length of string. Tape it to the bottom corner of the kite.

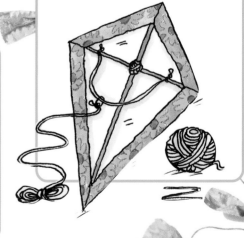

KITE HARNESS

Your kite will fly more easily if the string is attached to a harness, rather than tied straight to the kite.

How can I make loads of iron?

Miguel stares at the open fire that he uses as his furnace. It is a bowl-shaped hearth scraped out of the floor, where he heats iron ore and charcoal to make iron. But he cannot make enough iron this way. And his lord expects more and more heavy metal for armour.

Each day Miguel fills the hearth with hot coals and fans the flames to a great heat. He then heats the ore until the shiny metal in it melts. But it is a slow process and he can't make more iron than the furnace will produce.

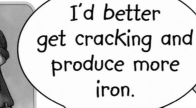

I'd better get cracking and produce more iron.

Miguel tries to add more iron ore to the furnace but it spills out and makes a horrible mess. He tries to find more furnaces but he can't. Now time is running out. His lord is getting impatient.

WHAT CAN HE DO?

- He could tell his lord he was ill with the plague. That would keep him away for a bit!

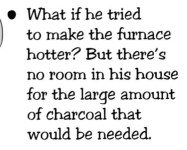

- He could steal some old bits of armour and melt them down. But it wouldn't make much of a difference.

- What if he tried to make the furnace hotter? But there's no room in his house for the large amount of charcoal that would be needed.

- Perhaps he could heat the furnace more effectively. He knows that when the wind blows over the furnace, it gets hotter.

I think I'll fix a gadget, just like the bellows used to make the castle fires burn more fiercely, to my furnace. It'll blow air over the coals. This will make them hotter and more efficient, so I can make more iron.

This sheepskin bellows blows air over the coals to make them glow hotter.

Smelting

Iron is a shiny metal that is made by heating iron ore, a mineral found in the ground. The first people to make iron from **ore** in this way were the Hittites, who lived in a part of Turkey from 1600 BC. During this period, it is thought that iron was more expensive than gold and silver. By AD1000, most of the world's civilisations knew how to make, or **smelt**, iron. In smelting, iron **ore** and **charcoal** are heated in the **furnace** until all the **oxygen** is removed from the ore. This process changes the ore into shiny iron. The iron is then heated again and hammered to remove any dirt. With a **bellows**, more air enters the furnace to heat the fire. This helps produce more iron.

Making heat

Burning is a way of making heat by a process called combustion. Combustion happens when a substance, such as wood, combines with the gas oxygen to give out heat as well as waste products. For example, when wood is burned, or combusts, the waste product is ash.

Oxygen must be present in the air for a substance to burn. Nothing will burn without oxygen. If the oxygen around a burning substance is used up, it will immediately stop burning. If you add more oxygen to a burning substance, you make it burn even harder. A bellows forces air, which contains oxygen, into a fire. This makes the fire flare up. A bellows is often used to help restart dying fires.

Hot molten metal is shaped by pouring it into moulds called forms. When the metal has cooled, the solid shapes can be removed.

ENERGY FROM BURNING

We burn fuel to give us light, heat or to power an engine. When a fuel such as petrol is burned, for example, it changes into a new substance. This kind of change that comes from burning creates energy. The energy stored in fuel is called chemical energy.

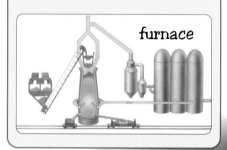

furnace

Inventor's words

bellows
charcoal
combustion
furnace
iron • ore
oxygen
smelt

Make a jelly hand

You will need

- cardboard
- plastic tray
- wooden canes
- elastic bands
- string
- bulldog clips
- rubber glove
- packet of green jelly

1 Make a 3-D cardboard platform with sloping sides. Cut an oblong hole in the centre for the tray.

2 Now glue 4 wooden canes to the outer edges of the platform.

3 Fix cross-section canes to the supporting canes by twisting elastic bands around the four corners.

4 Tie a piece of string to each corner of the frame and attach a bulldog clip to the other end.

5 Attach a rubber glove to the clips.

MAKE A MOULD

Make the jelly according the instructions on the packet and leave to cool. Fill up the glove with the jelly solution. Put it into the fridge to set, then carefully cut or peel away the glove. You have made a jelly hand!

39

How can I light up a huge cathedral?

Cuthbert looks at the plan of his new cathedral. It will be a magnificent building but he is afraid that it will be too dark. The bishop wants to decorate the cathedral with lots of wall hangings and pictures of Bible stories. How can Cuthbert decorate the cathedral and have enough light?

As the stone masons build the cathedral, Cuthbert marvels at their skills and the huge building they are constructing.

There's lots of room for murals and wall hangings, but he is worried that there is not enough light to show them off.

He thinks about changing the size of the windows. But the ones he designs now look big and ugly, and let in too much light. There's not enough room on the walls for the paintings and wall hangings.

What kind of windows will let in light but add to the beauty of the cathedral?

WHAT CAN HE DO?

- He could fill in the windows and light the cathedral with giant candles and bowls of fireflies.

- Maybe he could use his wall hangings to cover the windows. They would have to be moved to let in light.

- What if he painted pictures on boards and placed them across the windows? If he cut holes in the boards, the light would come through. But the pictures would be spoiled.

- How about using glass in the windows and painting the glass? The paint is too thick and blocks out the light. The pictures look beautiful, though.

I can use the glass for both light and decoration. I'll stain the glass in different colours while it is being made. Then I'll join together pieces of glass to make a colourful picture that will also let the light through.

Stained glass windows were used to tell a story as well as to let in light.

Stained glass

Although glass can be painted, real **stained glass** is coloured while the glass is being made. Colours are produced by adding metal oxides – metal combined with oxygen in a powder – to the other glass-making ingredients. Cobalt oxide makes blue glass while copper **oxide** makes red glass. The stained glass shines brightly when light shines through it.

Pieces of stained glass are joined with strips of lead to make windows. They are often seen in churches where pieces of glass are arranged to make a pattern or to tell Bible stories. This was important at a time when few people could read. Stained glass was probably first made in the Middle East, but by AD 500, simple stained glass was used in European churches.

White light

The colours that we see all come from a spectrum, or series, of colours that make up white light. Light is made up of waves that we can see with our eyes. But these waves do not all have the same wavelength. A wavelength is the distance between the crests, or tops, of the waves. Different wavelengths produce different colours, from violet to red.

Most objects either **absorb** or **reflect** back some of the waves of light. If they reflect all the wavelengths except the wavelength for green, we see the object as green. If they absorb all the wavelengths except the wavelength for yellow, we see the object as yellow.

When cobalt oxide is added to glass, the oxide absorbs all the lightwaves except the waves for blue, which it reflects back. So we see the glass shining blue as the light passes through it.

A rainbow occurs because water droplets act like prisms to break white light into the colours of the spectrum.

PRISM

A prism is a piece of triangular glass or plastic. When white light passes through it, the light breaks into the colours of the spectrum: red, orange, yellow, green, blue, indigo, and violet. This is because shorter wavelengths (violet) refract, or bend more than longer wavelengths (red).

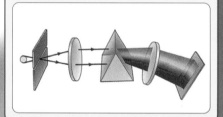

Inventor's words

absorb • oxide
reflect
refract
spectrum
stained glass
wavelength

Make a picture window

You will need

- white pencil
- black card
- scissors or craft knife
- coloured tissue paper
- glue
- sticky tape

1 With a white pencil, mark out patterns of flower shapes on pieces of black card.

2 Cut out the shapes, leaving a frame around each one.

3 Glue scraps of coloured tissue paper behind the spaces in each frame.

4 Tape your patterns on to a window so that the light shines through.

Glossary and index

Abacus Calculating machine with a frame on which wires strung with beads are stretched. Each bead represents a number, which can be moved on the wires to work out calculations.   p.25

Absorb How one substance takes in another substance. Some solids can absorb gases or liquids.   p.42

Altitude The height of an object above the earth's surface, or sea level.   p.5

Arabic numerals Numerals 1, 2, 3, etc, brought to Europe from Arabia around 1200, although originating in India.   p.26

Astrolabe Instrument used by astronomers and navigators to measure the altitude of stars and planets above the horizon.   p.5, 7

Astronomy Scientific study of all things in the Universe beyond the Earth's atmosphere. It is usually broken down into various fields, such as cosmology.   p.6

Axis Imaginary straight line that passes through the centre of an object. A rotating object, such as the Earth, turns on its axis.   p.10

Bellows Machine that forces air in a particular direction.   p.37, 38

Bow Front of a boat or ship.   p.13

Camera obscura Box camera with a small hole at one end that lets in light. The light creates an image on the opposite inside face of the box.   p.29

Charcoal Black solid that contains the element carbon. Charcoal can be made by burning wood.   p.37

Combustion To burn. When a substance combines with oxygen and is heated, it combusts, or burns.   p.38

Compass Instrument that helps people find their way from one place to another. A magnetic compass uses a pivoted magnetic needle that always aligns itself with Earth's magnetic north and south poles.   p.21, 23

Constellation Group of stars that make up a pattern or shape. Cancer, or the crab, is one of the constellations of the zodiac.   p.6

Equilibrium To be in balance. A set of scales is in equilibrium when both pans contain the same weight.   p.14

Furnace Device for creating heat. It can be used to heat homes or to make products.   p.36, 37

Fusion The joining together of two or more materials to make one substance.   p.17, 18

Glass Solid made by melting sand and fusing it with soda or potash and other chemical substances.   p.17

Gravity Force that pulls objects towards each other. Gravity causes objects to have weight.   p.14

Helm Tiller or wheel that controls a rudder.   p.13

Horizon Furthest point that an observer can see in any direction. It appears as a line where the Earth and the atmosphere meet. p.4, 5

Hub Middle part of a wheel that holds the axle. p.10

Image Replica, or copy, of a scene or object. You can see an image when you look in a mirror or when you take a photograph with a camera. p.29

Iron Chemical element. Iron is a dark grey metal found in the Earth's crust. Iron mixed with water becomes rust. p.36, 37

Kinetic energy The energy objects have when they are moving. The heavier or faster an object moves the more kinetic energy it has. p.34

Kite Type of flying craft made of material such as cloth or paper stretched over a frame. p.33, 34, 35

Lever Bar or rod that moves around a fulcrum. The effort of pressing down on one end lifts a load. p.10

Lightwaves Type of energy. They are electromagnetic waves that can be seen by human eyes. Lightwaves are found at the middle of the electromagnetic spectrum. p.30, 42

Lodestone Type of iron ore called magnetite that acts as a magnet. Early compasses used lodestone to find direction. p.21

Magnesium An element. Magnesium is a silvery-grey metal found in many minerals and in seawater. p.21

Magnet Object, usually of metal, that attracts other metal objects. It has a positive and negative pole. p.22, 23

Magnetic pole Point on the Earth's surface towards which a magnetic needle points. p.22

Melting point Temperature at which a solid melts. Mercury melts at $-39°$ C. p.18

Mixture Combination of substances. It can be a solid, liquid or gas. The substances in a mixture do not change each other. p.18

Molten Made liquid by melting. p.17

Numeral Symbol used to indicate a number, for example, the number five is shown by the numeral 5. p.26

Ore Type of mineral that is found in the Earth's crust. Ores are smelted to make metals such as copper and iron. p.37

Oxide Chemical compound containing a metal or non-metal that has been combined with oxygen. Rust is an oxide. p.41, 42

Oxygen Chemical element. It is a colourless gas that is found in the atmosphere. p.37, 38

Place value Value given to each column in a sequence of numerals. In the numeral sequence 15, the place value of the 5 is ones and the place value of the 1 is tens. So 15 is one ten and five ones; 25 would be two tens and five ones. p.26

Pole Part of a magnet. A bar magnet has a positive pole at one end and a negative pole at the other. Negative poles attract positive poles while positive poles attract negative poles. p.22

Potential energy Stored energy. Electrical energy in a battery is stored energy, or energy waiting to be used. p.34

Reflect A change in direction of electromagnetic waves. Lightwaves are reflected back when they hit a mirror. Radio waves can be reflected as an echo. p.30, 42

Refract To bend or change direction. Light waves can be refracted, or bent, by passing through a transparent object such as a lens or prism. p.42

Rudder Flat piece of wood or metal used to steer a ship or aeroplane. p.13, 15

Smelt To change an ore into a metal. Iron ore is smelted to become the metal iron. p.37

Spectrum Range of things sorted into a series. The electromagnetic spectrum sorts electromagnetic waves in series from those with the shortest wavelength, such as gamma rays, to those with the longest, such as radio waves. p.42

Spindle Part of a spinning machine. Thread is spun from fibre as the spindle turns. p.8, 9

Spinning Separating the tangled fibres in a boll (cotton) or fleece (wool) and turning them into yarn. p.8, 9

Stained glass Glass that is coloured while it is being made. p.41

Stern Rear end of a boat or ship. p.13

Tiller Bar used to turn a rudder. p.13

Unit First place in a place system indicating the number of ones. p.26

Universe All of space, including galaxies, stars and planets. Scientists believe the Universe extends out at least 13 billion light years. p.6

Vertical Direction that is straight up from the Earth's surface. p.5

Wavelength Distance between the peak of one electromagnetic wave and the peak of the next. p.42

Wheel Solid disk, or circular rim with spokes joined to a central hub. The hub turns round on an axle. p.8, 9, 10

Wheel and axle Simple machine used for lifting heavy objects. A wheel and axle mechanism is used in pulleys, water wells and cars. p.42

Wind energy Energy produced by the wind. Wind energy can be used to turn wheels with blades or sails. p.34

Tools and Materials

Almost all of the materials in this book can be found around the house or bought at your local art or craft shop. If you cannot find the exact item, try and replace it with something similar.

Most of the models will stick fast with PVA glue or even wallpaper paste. However, some materials need a stronger glue, so take care when using these as they may damage your clothes and even your skin. Ask an adult to help you.

Always protect furniture with newspaper or a large cloth, and cover your clothes by wearing an apron.

User Care

Take special care when handling sharp tools such as scissors, pointed gadgets, pieces of wire or craft knives. Ask an adult to help you when you need to use them.